D1318925

The Medieval World

Life on a Medieval anor

Marc Cels

 Crabtree Publishing Company
www.crabtreebooks.com

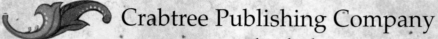

Crabtree Publishing Company

www.crabtreebooks.com

Coordinating editor: Ellen Rodger

Project editor: Carrie Gleason

Designer and production coordinator: Rosie Gowsell

Scanning technician: Arlene Arch-Wilson

Art director: Rob MacGregor

Project development, editing, photo editing, and layout:
First Folio Resource Group, Inc.: Tom Dart, Debbie Smith, Anikó Szocs

Proofreading: Lynne Elliott

Photo research: Maria DeCambra

Consultant: Isabelle Cochelin, University of Toronto

Photographs: Alinari/Art Resource, NY: p. 13 (bottom); Archivo Iconografico, S.A./Corbis/Magma: p. 22; Art Archive/Bodleian Library Oxford/Bodley 264 folio 246v: p. 31 (top); Art Archive/British Library: p. 8, p. 12 (top), p. 15 (top); Art Archive/Musée Calvet Avignon/Dagli Orti: p. 9, p. 27; British Library/Add. 19720 f.80: p. 18 (bottom); British Library/Add. 42130 f.158: p. 14 (top); British Library/Add. 42130 f.163v: p. 13 (top); British Library/Royal 20 C. VII f.60: p. 23; British Library/Topham-HIP/The Image Works: p. 16 (both), p. 18 (top); Christie's Images/Corbis/Magma: p. 25 (top); English Heritage/Topham-HIP/The Image Works: p. 19; Erich Lessing/Art Resource, NY: p. 17, p. 24 (bottom); HIP/Scala/Art Resource, NY: p. 29, p. 31 (bottom); The Illustrated London News Picture Library, London, UK/Bridgeman Art Library: title page; Mary Evans Picture Library: p. 25 (bottom); Museum voor Schone Kunsten, Ghent, Belgium, Giraudon/Bridgeman Art Library: p. 26; Réunion des Musées Nationaux/Art Resource, NY: p. 10; Scala/Art Resource, NY: cover, p. 12 (bottom), p. 30; Victoria & Albert Museum, London/Art Resource, NY: p. 5 (bottom left)

Map: Margaret Amy Reiach; Samara Parent

Illustrations: Jeff Crosby: pp. 6–7; Katherine Kantor: flags, title page (border), copyright page (bottom); Margaret Amy Reiach: borders, gold boxes, title page (illuminated letter), copyright page (top), contents page (background), pp. 4-5 (timeline), p. 4 (top), p. 11 (top right, middle, bottom left), p. 32 (all)

Cover: Summer was a busy season for medieval farmers living on the lord's manor. They worked together cutting hay to feed animals during the winter and shearing sheep's wool to make clothing.

Title page: Medieval peasants celebrated Christmas by going to church, feasting, singing, and dancing. Christmas carols began as lively outdoor circle dances with music and songs telling the story of how Jesus Christ was born.

Crabtree Publishing Company

www.crabtreebooks.com   1-800-387-7650

Cataloging-in-Publication data

Mark Cels
  Life on a Medieval Manor / written by Mark Cels.
     p. cm. -- (The medieval World)
  Includes index.
  ISBN 0-7787-1353-9 (RLB) -- ISBN 0-7787-1385-7 (pbk)
     1. Castles. 2. Manors. 3. Civilization, Medieval. I. Title.
II. Medieval worlds series
  GT3550.C412 2005
  390'.094--dc22
                              2004013061
                                 LC

**Published in
the United States**
PMB 16A
350 Fifth Ave.
Suite 3308
New York, NY
10118

**Published
in Canada**
616 Welland Ave.,
St. Catharines,
Ontario, Canada
L2M 5V6

**Published in the
United Kingdom**
73 Lime Walk
Headington
Oxford
0X3 7AD
United Kingdom

**Published
in Australia**
386 Mt. Alexander Rd.,
Ascot Vale (Melbourne)
V1C 3032

Table of Contents

In the Middle Ages

The Middle Ages, or the medieval period, began around 500 A.D. and lasted until around 1500 A.D. in western Europe. During this time, lords, such as kings and great nobles, controlled large areas of land. They gave smaller parcels of land, called manors, to loyal supporters.

Peasants, who made up a majority of the population, lived on and farmed the manor's land. In return for their labor, lords protected peasants from **invaders** and gave them a share of the land on which to grow their own crops and build small houses. This way of holding land is called manorialism.

On the Manor

Manors were made up of one or more villages. Each village had peasants' homes, a church, a mill where grain was ground into flour, ovens in which bread was baked, and a forge, where a blacksmith made horseshoes and iron tools. Sometimes, the lord's house was also in the village.

▼ *Medieval kings and nobles fought for control of Europe's rich farmlands. They gave loyal warriors, called knights, manors to rule in exchange for their help fighting. This system of ruling is called feudalism.*

Europeans begin using heavy plows, padded horse collars, and horseshoes **800s**		Use of windmills spreads **1100**	King Edward I of England decrees that all peasants could be called on to fight in a war **1285**	A disease called the Black Death kills one-third of Europe's population **1347–1349**
711 Arabs from North Africa introduce new crops, such as rice and watermelon, to Spain	**900s** Population begins to grow as food production increases; towns and trade grow	**1100s** Three-field system of farming becomes common in northern Europe		**1309–1325** Very poor weather causes crop failure, animal diseases, and famine

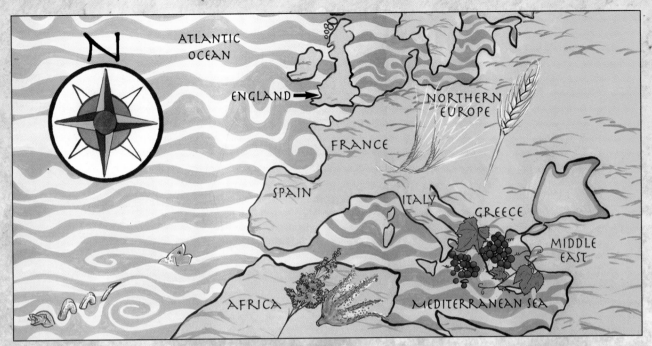

▲ *Most people in the Middle Ages lived in the countryside and made their living by farming. In the southern lands around the Mediterranean Sea, where the weather was hot and the soil was dry, wheat, olives, and grapes grew best. In the north, where the soil was heavy and wet and the weather was cooler, barley, rye, and oats were grown.*

Around the Village

Fields, meadows, and forests surrounded the village. Crops were planted in fields, **livestock** grazed in meadows, and forests provided wood for building, fuel for fires, and acorns to feed pigs. Nobles also hunted deer, boars, bears, and wolves in the forests. Nearby was a stream that supplied villagers with water.

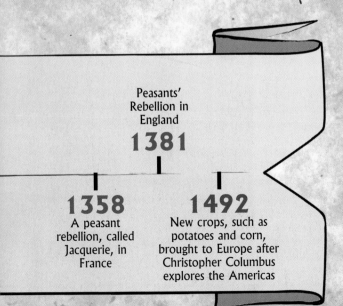

Peasants'
Rebellion in
England
1381

1358
A peasant
rebellion, called
Jacquerie, in
France

1492
New crops, such as
potatoes and corn,
brought to Europe after
Christopher Columbus
explores the Americas

▲ *Peasants harvested grain using simple tools, then carried the grain back to the village in a wagon.*

View of a Manor

Villages on the manor usually had populations of less than 600 people. The villagers produced almost everything they needed, including food, clothing, and farming tools. Peasants rarely journeyed off the manor. When they did, it was to trade or sell their produce in neighboring villages and towns, or to buy supplies.

1. Peasants lived in wattle and daub homes, with roofs thatched with a thick layer of straw, reeds, and other plants. The homes were painted with a white substance called lime that protected them from rain.

2. Peasant farmers had strips of land in each field.

3. The church, where peasants worshiped and held community events, was at the center of the village.

4. Only nobles were allowed to hunt in the manor's forests.

5. The manor house, where the lord and his family lived, was surrounded by other buildings, such as stables, storage sheds, and the kitchen. The kitchen was outside the main building in case of fire.

6. The mill, where grain was ground into flour, was powered by water from the river running through the village.

7. Livestock grazed in pastures that the villagers shared.

Peasants' Lives

Peasants worked from sunrise to sunset growing food and making other products for their families, for their lords, and for sale to towns. Most peasants were serfs. Serfs, or villeins, were not allowed to leave the manor without the lord's permission. Other peasants were free peasants, able to move away if they chose to.

Serfs and Free Peasants

Serfs were given land for a house and a yard, as well as strips in the field on which to grow food for their families. In return, they had to farm the lord's land, called his demesne. Serfs also had to keep the village in good repair, which included repairing bridges, clearing roads, and maintaining buildings. Serfs paid the lord many different fees, rents, and fines if they broke the law.

Free peasants rented land from the lord, paying him a portion of their farm produce or a cash rent. Free peasants did not have to work the lord's demesne, nor did they have to pay as many fines, rents, and fees as serfs did.

Beginning in the 1100s, peasants **cultivated** more land and grew more crops as farming tools improved. Some serfs earned enough money selling extra produce to buy their way out of serfdom and become free. Lords used the money free peasants paid them to hire peasant laborers to work their demesne.

▲ *Peasants who did not have land were hired by lords or wealthier peasants to do farmwork, such as picking fruit, or to work as servants.*

Peasants' Houses

In southern Europe, most peasant families lived in small homes made of stone, with roofs covered with clay tiles or stone shingles. In the north, most peasants lived in homes made of a framework of woven twigs called wattle. The wattle was covered with daub, a mixture of mud, straw, and animal dung.

Peasant houses had hard dirt floors covered with cut reeds or straw. There were only a few pieces of furniture, including a bench or stools, a **trestle** table, and a storage chest. At night, the furniture was moved aside and the family slept on straw mattresses on the floor. Smoked hams and sausages hung from roof beams away from mice and other animals.

Peasant Food

Peasants usually ate meals of heavy, dark bread and pottage, a thick soup made by slowly boiling grains in water. Pottage was flavored with beans or peas, vegetables, herbs, bones, and small amounts of bacon or salted pork. In summer, peasants cooked vegetables that they grew in their gardens. Cabbages, carrots, and turnips were kept fresh in cool, dark places and were eaten for most of winter. Peasants ate very little meat because it was expensive to keep animals. Chicken and small amounts of salted beef and pork were considered treats.

▼ *Peasants cooked most of their meals in metal pots called cauldrons. Cauldrons were heated on iron stands over fires. Large cauldrons were used to prepare soups and stews for gatherings of friends and family.*

Farming the Land

Peasant work followed the cycle of the seasons. In spring, peasants planted summer crops, put animals out to graze in the pasture, and made cheese and butter from cows' milk. In summer, peasants cut hay in the meadows and sheared sheep of their wool.

Autumn was the busiest time as peasants harvested the summer crops. Early in winter, peasants plowed the winter fields and planted spring crops. Livestock were slaughtered in winter and their meat preserved by salting or smoking it.

Dividing the Land

In the early Middle Ages, a manor's farmland was divided into two fields. One field was planted with crops. The other field was left fallow, or unplanted, so that the soil could regain its **nutrients**. By the 1100s, farmlands in northern Europe were divided into three fields instead of two. One field was planted with rye and wheat early in winter. The second field was planted with barley, oats, peas, and beans in the early spring. The third field was left fallow. This way, more crops were grown.

▼ *Late in autumn, peasants led pigs to the forest to feed on acorns, which were being harvested.*

Growing Wheat

The most important crops that peasants grew were cereal grains, such as wheat and rye. These were the main sources of food for people in the Middle Ages.

▼ A heavy wooden frame with iron teeth, called a harrow, was dragged along the field to break up the soil.

▶ The farmer sowed, or planted, grain by scattering seeds on plowed soil.

◀ When the grain was golden and ripe, it was reaped, or cut by hand, with curved knives called sickles. The stems were tied together into sheaves and carted back to a barn in the village.

▼ Grain was stored in a granary to keep it dry and protect it from mice and other animals. Some of the grain was put aside to be used as seed for the next planting.

▶ The grain was beaten out of the sheaves of wheat with sticks called flails. Then, the light, inedible husks of grain, called chaff, were blown away with a handheld fan, leaving the heavier grain kernels behind.

New Technology

The heavy, wet soil of northern Europe was difficult to farm. In the 800s, peasants started using heavy plows to make their work easier. The plows were made of wood and had iron blades that cut through the soil. The soil was pushed to the side, leaving a trench in which seeds were planted.

At first, teams of oxen were used to pull plows. By the 900s, peasants hitched faster-moving horses to plows using horse collars. Horse collars had been invented in China. Iron horseshoes allowed horses to move easily through the moist soil and protected their hooves. Plows and the animals that pulled them were expensive, so peasants shared them.

▲ A skilled plowman guided the plow while another peasant led the team of oxen. It was hard to turn the heavy plow, so fields were plowed in long strips so less turns were needed.

Farming in the Arab World

In the **Arab** lands of the Middle East and Spain, farmers planted fields of wheat, barley, and a cereal grass called sorghum. They also grew crops that were less familiar to farmers in western Europe, such as eggplant, sugar cane, and cotton. Grapes, olives, almonds, apricots, lemons, oranges, and figs grew in vineyards and orchards, all watered with **irrigation** channels.

▶ *At harvest time, ripe olives were shaken or beaten out of trees with sticks, then picked off the ground. Olives were either stored for eating later or they were pressed to remove their oil for cooking or burning in lamps.*

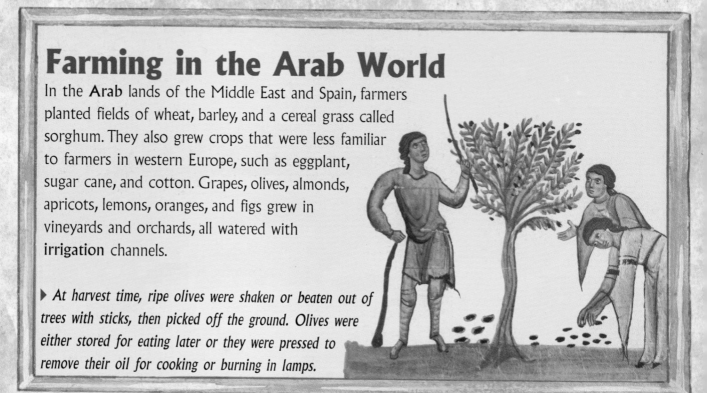

Raising Farm Animals

Peasants in the Middle Ages raised sheep, using their wool to make cloth, their hides to make **parchment** for writing, and their meat for food. Pigs were valued for their meat. Cows were raised for their milk, which was used to make cheese and butter, for their meat, and for their hides, which were turned into leather. Chickens and geese provided eggs and meat, and goose feathers were used to stuff bedding.

Livestock was sometimes kept inside peasants' homes. The animals were noisy and smelly, but their body heat helped warm the house in winter. Other peasants kept livestock in a hut attached to the house or in a separate building.

▲ *When sheep were brought in from pasture, they were kept in a sheepfold, which was a pen woven from sticks.*

Fishing

Fish was an important food across Europe because **Christians** were forbidden from eating meat on Fridays and during Lent, the 40 days before **Easter**. Many peasants on sea coasts made their living fishing for herring and cod. The fish was dried or packed in salt, to be eaten later or traded to lands farther from the sea.

◀ *Villagers netted fish, such as carp or eels, in lakes and rivers, or they raised fish in ponds.*

Tradespeople

Some villagers worked at trades. Many trades were related to farming, such as making farming tools or turning farm products into useful items such as cloth.

Millers ▶

Peasant women carried grain to the lord's mill in sacks. A miller ground the grain into flour between two flat, heavy stones called millstones. The power to turn the millstones came from wind or water from a nearby stream. To use the mill, peasants had to pay the miller a share of their flour. Peasants could be fined if they used a hand-turned mill at home.

◀ Bakers

Peasants sometimes brought their bread dough to the manor's oven to be baked. The baker used a long, wooden paddle to place the loaves of dough in a large stone, brick, or clay oven. In return, the peasants had to give the baker some of their loaves of bread. Peasants who baked bread at home could be fined by the lord.

Smiths ▶

Blacksmiths made and repaired iron tools and horseshoes. They softened the iron in forges, which were ovens heated by **charcoal**. To make fires burn very hot, they pumped air into forges with **bellows**. Then, smiths hammered the hot iron into shape on iron blocks called anvils. Manor forges were built and owned by lords, and peasants paid smiths for their work.

◀ Carpenters

Carpenters built wooden buildings and furniture, and made and repaired wooden tools. They used axes, saws, knives, and chisels to cut and carve wood. Holes were made with drills that were cranked with a handle. Boards were shaved smooth and flat with sharp planes.

Medieval Surnames

In the early Middle Ages, most peasants were known by only one name. Surnames, or last names, started to be used in the 1200s. Many surnames told about a person's trade:

- ▶ Carter: someone who drives a cart
- ▶ Cartwright: someone who makes and repairs carts
- ▶ Chapman: a merchant
- ▶ Cooper: a barrel maker
- ▶ Fletcher: an arrow maker

- ▶ Smith: a metal worker
- ▶ Tanner: someone who makes leather from animal hides
- ▶ Taylor: someone who makes clothes
- ▶ Thatcher: someone who makes roofs from straw or reeds

Women and Children

Peasant women spent much of their time caring for young children, making clothes, and preparing meals. They also tended their home gardens, looked after chickens, sheared sheep, milked cows, and helped out in the fields.

Medieval women gave birth at home without doctors to help them. It was not unusual for a mother and her baby to die during a difficult birth. Even if the birth went well, many children died at a young age because of illnesses and accidents.

Making Clothes

Peasant women made cloth and clothing from wool or from the linen fibers of the flax plant. Men wore long shirts, called tunics, with stockings or hose. Stockings were long socks that came up past the knees. Hose went right up to the waist. Women wore long-sleeved linen dresses, called chemises, as underwear. Over top, they wore wool tunics with sleeves, then sleeveless surcoats with open sides. Peasants only had one or two sets of clothes, which women patched and mended as they became worn or torn.

In the late 1200s, women in Europe began using spinning wheels to spin wool into thread and yarn.

Children at Work

Young peasant children played around their homes with simple toys, such as tops, whistles, hobby horses, carts, and dolls, that their parents made. At about seven years of age, they began to help with chores. Children herded geese, scared birds away from newly planted fields, gathered fruit and nuts, and collected eggs from chickens. Boys learned how to work in the fields and care for animals, or they learned their fathers' trades, such as milling or blacksmithing. Some parents paid a **priest** to teach their sons to read and write. Girls were taught to cook and preserve food, make clothing, tend gardens, and care for animals. They also learned how to make medicines from wild plants or from herbs growing in their gardens.

Older Children

By the age of twelve or fourteen, children were doing adult work in the fields and around the house. A few young people worked as servants in the lord's house. Boys worked in kitchens as turnspits or scullions, roasting meat over fires or washing dishes. Girls served as maids, cleaning, doing laundry, and mending clothes.

▼ *Peasant children played games such as tag or leapfrog, rocked on barrels, and invented other ways to have fun.*

The Lord

Most manors were ruled by lords who were knights, but some manors were ruled by the Church or by monasteries. Most lords had more than one manor. The lords' wealth came from the food, rents, fines, and fees they collected from the peasants.

A Lord's Duties

The lord's main duty was to fight for his overlord and advise him about important matters, such as when to go to war. If a lord failed to be loyal to his overlord or did not perform his duties, the overlord took back his land and gave it to someone else.

A lord with only one manor managed it himself. He supervised peasants' work, collected fees, taxes, and rents, punished minor crimes, and settled disputes.

The lord's wife, the lady of the manor, supervised servants, checked household accounts, paid expenses, and entertained guests. She also ran the manor when her husband was away.

▶ Serfs and peasant laborers planted this lord's demesne with grape vines. The grapes were pressed into wine, which the lord enjoyed at meals or sold to wine merchants.

▲ After King William I conquered England in 1066, he had his men record the value of the land and equipment on every manor. The information was gathered into the Domesday Book so William knew how much tax he could collect from his kingdom.

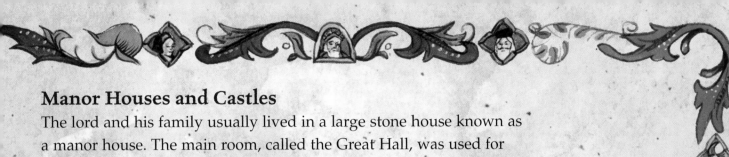

Manor Houses and Castles

The lord and his family usually lived in a large stone house known as a manor house. The main room, called the Great Hall, was used for meetings and as a dining room for the lord, his family, and important guests. Manor houses often had a prayer room called a chapel. A room above the Great Hall, called a solar, served as a bedroom and living room for the lord and his family. Near the manor house were other buildings, such as a kitchen, a bakehouse, stables, and barns. There was also a garden and fruit orchard.

Lords showed their wealth and importance by dressing in beautiful clothes made of fine fabrics. They served delicious feasts of roasted meats and fish flavored with expensive spices. Acrobats, dancers, and musicians who sang poems and songs about brave knights and beautiful ladies entertained the nobles as they dined.

▼ *Manor houses often had stairs on the outside leading up to the solar. Peasants only entered manor houses if they were servants or to attend the manor court.*

Running the Manor

Lords who had large manors usually did not have the time or interest to manage their land themselves. Instead, they hired several people to help them. The lord's most important assistants were the steward, the bailiff, and the reeve.

The Steward ▸

A lord with more than one manor appointed a steward, also called a seneschal, to supervise all his manors. The steward visited the manors two or three times a year. He kept account of each manor's money, presided over the manor court for the lord, and hired other officers, such as bailiffs and reeves, to help him.

◂ The Bailiff

The steward chose a bailiff to be the lord's **representative** on a manor. The bailiff was usually a younger son from a **lesser noble** family or the son of a wealthy peasant family. He made sure that everyone followed the manor's laws, but most of his time was spent managing the lord's demesne. He decided what to plant and when, and he organized work that involved the whole village, such as harvesting. He also hired peasants and skilled craftspeople to repair buildings, make tools, and do other kinds of work. If anything was needed that the peasants could not make or produce, the bailiff bought it from a nearby town.

The Reeve ▶

The reeve was a wealthy peasant chosen by the other peasants to help the bailiff. He kept a very careful account of all the crops, animals, and other produce from the manor, checking that nothing had been stolen. He also kept track of how much rent and work the peasants owed the lord. Reeves were usually unable to read or write, so they kept count by cutting marks into tally sticks.

◀ The Reeve's Assistants

A beadle, or hayward, helped the reeve by collecting fines and rents from peasants and ensuring that serfs did the work that they owed the lord. In addition, the beadle was responsible for saving and storing seed that would be planted on the lord's demesne the following year. Sometimes, a woodward was hired to guard the manor woods from **poachers**, since only the lord had the right to hunt animals in the forest. Peasant women were appointed as **ale** tasters to make sure that the manor's ale was of a good quality and was sold at the correct price.

The Manor Court

A few times a year, the lord or his steward presided over the manor court. The manor court was held inside the manor house, or outside under a tree during the summer.

Some cases, such as those involving marriages, were tried by judges in Church courts, according to religious laws.

The villagers elected up to twelve serfs as **jurors** to settle disputes and decide on fines for peasants who broke the manor's rules. Their decisions were written down by the steward's **clerk** in records, called manor rolls, which also included the manor's laws. The manor rolls were used to help decide on later punishments.

Fees and Fines

At the court, the reeve or bailiff announced the names of peasants owing fees or fines. One type of fee was called a tallage, which was an annual payment that a serf paid to the lord. Another fee, called woodsilver, was a peasant's payment to the lord for allowing him to take wood out of the manor's forest. Serfs who failed to pay their full fees or do their share of work on the lord's demesne were fined by the court.

Disputes

Peasants brought their disputes before the manor court. For example, if two peasants claimed ownership of the same strip of land in a field or if peasants complained that their neighbors' livestock trampled their crops, they went to court. Sometimes, peasants accused their bailiff or reeve of asking them to do too much work. The manor court decided who was right and who was owed money in such disputes.

▲ *Serious crimes, such as murder or stealing from the Church, were tried in the courts of great nobles or kings. People found guilty were often dragged away by guards and executed by hanging.*

Crimes

The manor court also dealt with more serious crimes, such as theft or fighting. People guilty of these crimes were sometimes punished by shaming. They had their legs and hands locked in **stocks** in a public place, or they were stripped of their clothes and walked through the village for everyone to see.

Manors did not have police, so every peasant was responsible for keeping law and order. If a serious crime was detected, peasants raised a hue and cry, which means they shouted for assistance. Everyone who heard was expected to help. Then, the peasants turned over the criminal to the beadle, reeve, or bailiff.

Manor Rolls

A few manor rolls survive from medieval England. They indicate the fines paid for various crimes. The fines were paid in silver pennies, the main **currency** of the Middle Ages. A peasant laborer in the late 1200s earned about two pennies a day.

The following are some examples of fines:
▶ Six pennies for not plowing the lord's land or for plowing the land poorly
▶ Twelve pennies for pretending to be sick and not working for the lord
▶ Six pennies for letting one's livestock trample the lord's grain
▶ Twelve pennies for making ale too weak and selling it before it was tasted
▶ Six pennies for wounding a neighbor
▶ Four shillings (48 pennies) for not looking after one's elderly mother

The Church

In the Middle Ages, most Europeans were Christians. Christians believe in one God and follow the teachings of Jesus Christ, who they believe is the son of God.

The church was usually the largest building in a village and was the center of life for the people who lived there. Villagers went to church to pray every Sunday, on holy days, and to mark important times in their lives. Babies were **baptized**, couples were married, and the dead were buried at the church.

▲ *A couple married by saying their wedding vows at the church's front door. There was only one wedding ring, given by the man to the woman. The wedding was usually followed by a feast with dancing and music.*

◀ *Village churches had a tower called a steeple in which a bell was hung. A rope was pulled to ring the bell and call people to pray or to announce the death of a villager. The sound of bells was also believed to frighten away evil spirits and storms.*

A Meeting Place

Villagers also used the church as a place for community meetings and a place to do business. Markets and gatherings, such as church ales, were often held in the square, or lawn, in front of the church. Church ales were parties at which food and drink were sold to pay for repairs or renovations to the church.

Priests

The priest was one of the most important members of the community. He led church services in Latin, the language used by the Church, and explained the Bible and the Church's teachings in the peasants' everyday language. The priest also performed religious ceremonies, the most important of which was Mass. During Mass, the villagers watched as the priest said a prayer over special bread, called the host, and wine. The priest also taught people how to live good lives and he gave them advice.

The lord usually hired the village priest and gave him a good house and piece of land for farming and raising animals. The priest earned money by being paid for baptisms, marriages, and burial services.

▲ *Peasants lined up to pay the Church a tax called a tithe. The tithe was one-tenth of all the crops and animals they produced.*

Training to Be a Priest

Boys wishing to become priests began their training by helping the village priest. They learned prayers and hymns, lit candles, rang bells, and followed the priest in religious **processions.** When they were older, boys studied at **cathedral** schools in towns.

▶ *Priests performing Mass or other ceremonies wore special clothes, called vestments.*

25

Celebrations

Peasants rested from their hard work by joyfully celebrating festivals. The festivals were usually religious celebrations, many of which also marked the change of seasons. Manors in different countries had their own holiday customs, which included feasts, parades, games, dancing, and singing.

Christmas

Christmas, on December 25, celebrates the birth of Jesus Christ. On Christmas, peasants in the Middle Ages went to church for special services, decorated their homes with greenery, such as holly and mistletoe, and sang carols that told the story of Jesus' birth. The Christmas season ended on Plow Monday, early in January. Peasants took their plows to church so the priest could bless them at the start of spring plowing.

Easter

Easter, in March or April, was the holiest time of the year. It honored the day that Jesus rose from the dead after being crucified, or put to death on a cross. People went to church at Easter for a special Mass.

Easter was also the time to celebrate the end of winter. There were feasts of roast lamb and eggs, and games played with eggs colored with vegetable dyes. Children and adults tried rolling their eggs in straight lines or tapping them against someone else's egg to see whose was the strongest.

▼ *Celebrations included lively dancing outdoors to the music of pipes, drums, and other instruments that peasants made at home.*

Saints' Days

Each village had a patron **saint** who villagers believed watched over them and protected them from harm. Villagers honored their saint on a special day, called a saint's day. On saints' days, villagers went to church and paraded around the village with pictures or statues of the saint. At night, there was a church ale with singing, dancing, and eating.

◀ *It was a special honor to carry the saint's statue during a saint's day parade. Processions often went out into the fields, where crops were blessed and villagers sang songs praising the saints.*

Celebrating the Seasons

May Day, on May 1, celebrated spring. At midnight, young men and women went to the woods and fields blowing whistles and horns. They returned with flowers and branches of green leaves to decorate their homes. A village girl was chosen May Queen and crowned with a wreath of flowers. She led the villagers in songs, games, and dances around a pole, called a Maypole, that was decorated with ribbons and garlands.

The Feast of Saint John the Baptist, on June 24, honored Jesus' cousin and celebrated Mid Summer, the time of year when summer nights are shortest and days longest. Peasants sang and danced in a circle around a large bonfire at night. As the fire died down, men leaped over it for good luck.

Lammas, on August 1, marked the beginning of the grain harvest. The word Lammas means "Loaf Mass" because the first ripened grain and the first loaf of bread were brought to church to thank God for a good harvest.

A Difficult Life

In the Middle Ages, peasants faced many hardships. They worked long days doing difficult labor to feed their families and pay their lords. Sometimes, there was not enough food to eat. Peasants also suffered from injuries and diseases for which there were no cures or medicines.

Famine

Many peasants produced just enough food for their families, their lords, and the Church. If crops were damaged because of poor weather or disease, there was a danger of **famine**. From 1309 to 1325, Europe experienced famines due to cool, wet weather. Grains did not ripen or they grew moldy in the fields. Without enough to eat, farm animals became sick and peasants starved.

Diseases

In the Middle Ages, the only medicines available were made from wild plants and herbs. These did not cure serious diseases, such as the Plague, also called the Black Death.

In 1347, the Plague arrived in Europe, carried by rats on trading ships. Infected fleas living on the rats spread the disease to humans. There were two types of plagues. The bubonic plague caused large black bumps under people's arms or on their necks. When the bumps broke open, they oozed blood and puss. The pneumonic plague infected the lungs and caused people to develop fevers, spit blood, sweat, and cough. About one-third of the population died over three years, and manors were left without enough workers.

▲ *Doctors tried to protect themselves from catching the Plague by wearing special clothing.*

Peasant Rebellions

During the 1300s and 1400s, peasants in many parts of Europe **rebelled** against their worsening conditions. The Jacquerie rebellion took place in France in 1358. Peasants and townspeople were angry when they were forced to pay a tax to help pay for France's war with England. Peasants were also angry that their lords did not protect them from English soldiers who destroyed their villages. French peasants attacked the lords and burned down the manor houses. The rebellion was eventually crushed by an army of French knights who killed thousands of peasants and burned down villages. The bodies of rebels were hung from trees as a warning to other peasants.

In 1381, the Peasants' Rebellion broke out in England. Peasants were angry that after the Black Death, English lords forced them to work even harder than before without raising their wages. As well, everyone over the age of fifteen had to pay a tax for the king's war against France. Peasants attacked tax collectors, burned the houses of royal officials, and murdered members of the government. The rebels demanded that the king be their only lord, that all the property of the Church be given to the peasants, and that serfs be granted freedom. The king promised to help, but when the peasants went home, 200 rebel leaders were hanged.

▼ *Richard II was king of England during the Peasants' Rebellion. The king had the rebel leader killed and told the peasant army to go home.*

Growing Towns

Towns began to grow as centers of trade in the 900s. Peasants sold extra fruits and vegetables, animals, and wool at town markets. Leather goods, tools, and other supplies were bought from townspeople who had set up shops. Lords or their servants visited towns to purchase expensive fabrics, spices, and other goods from faraway countries.

In the later Middle Ages, many peasants moved to towns. Serfs who ran away from their manors became free if they stayed in a town for a year and a day. Other serfs bought their freedom and left the manor.

▼ *Unlike village peasants, most townspeople did not produce their own food. They bought fresh fruit, vegetables, eggs, milk, meat, and bread from villagers who sold their goods at town markets. The markets were usually held once a week.*

Life in Towns

Peasants entered towns through gates and passed through narrow, crooked streets on their way to markets and shops. Stone and wooden houses stood close to one another, with craftspeople's shops on the ground floor. Garbage and sewage were thrown into the streets. The smell was terrible until laws were finally passed to keep towns clean.

▲ *Towns were often built along rivers or the sea so that merchants could bring goods from distant lands by boat. High walls protected towns from invaders.*

Town Charters

At first, towns were ruled by lords, who made laws and collected taxes from townspeople. In the later Middle Ages, lords in some parts of Europe, such as England, gave towns their freedom with written documents called town charters. A charter described the rights and duties of the townspeople. Towns with charters could make their own laws governing business, trade, and markets and raise their own taxes for building walls and other needs. In exchange for granting charters, lords received a yearly payment of cash.

In other parts of Europe, such as France, becoming independent was not as easy. Sometimes, there was violence as towns struggled to gain freedom from their lords.

◀ *In 1215, King John of England granted this charter to the people of London, giving them the right to choose their own mayor each year.*

Glossary

ale An alcoholic drink made from grain

Arab Related to the Middle East

baptize To dip a person in water during a ceremony that receives him or her into the Christian Church

bellows A tool that blows air when pulled open and squeezed closed

cathedral The main church of a district, led by a bishop

charcoal A black substance found in nature that is used as fuel

Christian A person who follows the religion of Christianity. Christians believe in one God, and follow the teachings of Jesus Christ, who they believe is God's son

clerk A person who keeps records and accounts

cultivate To prepare land for crops by plowing soil

currency Money

Easter The holiday that celebrates the day Jesus Christ rose from the dead after being put to death on a cross

famine An extreme shortage of food

harvest To gather crops from fields

invader A person who enters another's land to conquer or steal

irrigation A system of supplying land with water

juror A person who serves on a jury. The jury hears evidence in a court of law and reaches a decision about another person's guilt or innocence based on the evidence

lesser noble A noble whose family is less important or wealthy than other noble families

livestock Farm animals

merchant A person who buys and sells goods

monastery The place where a community of monks or nuns live and work

nutrient A substance that living things need in order to grow

parchment A writing material made from sheep's skin

poacher A person who hunts or fishes unlawfully on private property

priest A person who leads religious ceremonies in the Catholic Church

procession A line of people walking forward in a ceremony

rebel To disobey or fight against authority

representative A person who is chosen to make decisions for other people

saint A holy person, according to the Christian Church

stocks A wooden frame with holes in it that held a criminal's hands and feet in place

trestle A frame that supports a tabletop

Index

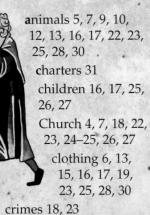
1 2 3 4 5 6 7 8 9 0 Printed in the U.S.A. 0 9 8 7 6 5 4